# THE POWER OF POSITIVE THINKING

## TRANSFORM YOUR LIFE WITH A POSITIVE MINDSET

FAVOUR UZOUKWU

ISBN-13: 979-8-8842-9345-8

# DEDICATION

This book is dedicated to all those who believe in the power of positivity and strive to cultivate a mindset of hope, resilience, and gratitude. May these pages inspire you to embrace life's challenges with courage and optimism, and may you discover the endless possibilities within the realm of positive thinking.

# CONTENTS

# INTRODUCTION

In a world often filled with challenges and uncertainties, the power of positive thinking stands out as a beacon of hope and resilience. It's not about ignoring life's difficulties or wearing rose-colored glasses; rather, it's a mindset that enables you to approach life's ups and downs with a constructive attitude. This book is a guide to understanding the transformative power of positive thinking and how it can profoundly impact your life. Being positive doesn't just mean having optimistic thoughts; it's making the deliberate decision to see the good things in life, especially when faced with hardship. Research has shown that maintaining a positive outlook can have a profound effect on your mental and physical health. It can reduce stress, boost your immune system, increase your lifespan, and improve your overall quality of life. In this book, we'll explore the science behind positive thinking, its many benefits, and practical strategies for incorporating it into your daily life. From cultivating gratitude to practicing mindfulness, you'll learn how to nurture a positive mindset that can help you navigate life's challenges with grace and optimism. So, are you ready to embark on a journey of self-discovery and empowerment? Let's dive in and explore the incredible power of positive thinking.

# CHAPTER TWO

# *Understanding Positive Thinking*

Positive thinking is more than just a feel-good mantra; it's a mindset that can profoundly impact every aspect of your life. At its core, positive thinking involves focusing on the good in any given situation and approaching challenges with a constructive attitude. In this chapter, we'll delve deeper into what positive thinking is and explore its many benefits.

### What is Positive Thinking?

Positive thinking is a mental attitude that involves focusing on the positive aspects of life and expecting positive outcomes. It's about approaching life's challenges with a sense of optimism and resilience, even when faced with difficulties. Positive thinking is not about ignoring reality or denying the existence of problems; rather, it's about acknowledging challenges while maintaining a hopeful and proactive attitude.

### The Science Behind Positive Thinking

Research has shown that thinking positively can greatly improve the health of both your mind and body. Positive thoughts can trigger the release of neurotransmitters like serotonin and dopamine, which are known as "feel-good" chemicals that contribute to feelings of happiness and well-being. These neurotransmitters can help reduce stress and anxiety, improve mood, and enhance overall mental health.

Better physical health has also been connected to positive thinking. Research indicates that individuals with an optimistic attitude on life have a lower risk of developing certain health issues, such as cardiovascular disease, and may even have longer lifespans than those with a more pessimistic outlook.

*Benefits of Positive Thinking*

The benefits of positive thinking are far-reaching and can impact every area of your life. Some of the key benefits include:

*Improved mental health*: Positive thinking can reduce symptoms of depression and anxiety, improve self-esteem, and enhance overall emotional well-being.

*Better physical health*: Positive thinking can boost the immune system, reduce the risk of developing chronic diseases, and promote overall physical well-being.

*Enhanced relationships*: Positive thinking can improve communication skills, foster empathy, and compassion, and strengthen interpersonal relationships.

*Increased resilience*: Positive thinking can help you cope with stress, bounce back from setbacks, and adapt to change more easily.

In the following chapters, we'll explore practical strategies for cultivating a positive mindset and incorporating positive thinking into your daily life. By understanding the science behind positive thinking and its many benefits, you can begin to harness its power to transform your life for the better.

# CHAPTER THREE

# *The Benefits of Positive Thinking*

Positive thinking is not just a feel-good concept; it can have tangible benefits that impact every aspect of your life. In this chapter, we'll explore some of the key benefits of positive thinking and how it can enhance your overall well-being.

### *Improved Mental Health*

The influence of positive thinking on mental health is among its most important advantages. Positive thoughts can help reduce symptoms of depression and anxiety, improve self-esteem, and enhance overall emotional well-being. By focusing on the positive aspects of life, you can train your mind to see the good in every situation, even during difficult times.

### *Better Physical Health*

Positive thinking has also been linked to improved physical health. Studies have shown that people who maintain a positive outlook are less likely to develop certain health conditions, such as cardiovascular disease, and may even live longer than those who have a more negative outlook on life. Positive thoughts can boost the immune system, reduce inflammation, and promote overall physical well-being.

### *Enhanced Relationships*

Positive thinking can also improve your relationships with others. By maintaining a positive attitude, you can improve your communication skills, foster empathy, and compassion, and strengthen your interpersonal relationships. People are naturally drawn to positive individuals, and cultivating a positive mindset can help you build deeper, more meaningful connections with others.

*Increased Resilience*

Another important benefit of positive thinking is that it makes you stronger. An upbeat attitude makes it easier for people to get back on their feet faster after something bad happens and adapt to change more easily. By maintaining a positive outlook, you can build the resilience needed to navigate life's challenges with grace and optimism.

*Incorporating Positive Thinking into Your Life*

To reap the benefits of positive thinking, it's important to incorporate it into your daily life. This can be done through practices such as gratitude journaling, positive self-talk, and mindfulness meditation. By making positivity a habit, you can train your mind to focus on the good in every situation and reap the many benefits of a positive mindset.

# CHAPTER FOUR

# *Cultivating a Positive Mindset*

To cultivate a positive mindset, it's essential to practice habits and adopt attitudes that promote positivity. In this section, we'll talk about some easy ways to think positively as part of our daily health and wellness habits.

*Practicing Gratitude*

Being thankful is a strong way to think positively. By focusing on the things, you're thankful for, you can shift your perspective from what's lacking in your life to what you have. Keeping a gratitude journal, where you write down things, you're grateful for each day, can help you cultivate a habit of gratitude and train your mind to focus on the positive.

*Positive Self-Talk*

The way you talk to yourself has a significant impact on your mindset. Negative self-talk can reinforce feelings of self-doubt and inadequacy, while positive self-talk can boost your confidence and self-esteem. Practice replacing negative thoughts with positive affirmations and statements that empower you. For example, instead of saying, "I can't do this," say, "I am capable, and I can overcome this challenge."

*Mindfulness and Meditation*

Mindfulness and meditation are practices that can help you stay present and focused on the moment. They can also help you become more aware of your thoughts and feelings, allowing you to recognize negative thought patterns and replace them with more positive ones. Regular meditation practice can help reduce stress and anxiety, improve your mood, and cultivate a sense of inner peace and positivity.

*Surrounding Yourself with Positive Influences*

Your perspective can be greatly influenced by the individuals you choose to surround yourself with. Surround yourself with positive, supportive people who uplift you and encourage you to be your best self. Reduce the number of negative influences in your life that might sap your vitality and stifle your optimism, such as unfavorable news or poisonous relationships.

By incorporating these practices into your daily life, you can cultivate a positive mindset that will help you approach life's challenges with optimism and resilience. Remember, positivity is a choice, and by choosing to focus on the good in every situation, you can transform your life for the better.

# CHAPTER FIVE

# *The Power of Visualization and Affirmations*

Visualization and affirmations are powerful tools that can help reinforce positive thinking and empower you to achieve your goals. In this chapter, we'll explore how visualization and affirmations work and how you can use them to enhance your positive mindset.

*How Visualization Reinforces Positive Thinking*

Visualization is the practice of creating a mental image of a desired outcome or goal. By visualizing your goals as already accomplished, you can train your mind to focus on positive outcomes and increase your belief in your ability to achieve them. Visualization works by activating the same neural pathways in your brain that are activated when you perform the actions you're visualizing, helping to strengthen the connections in your brain related to that goal.

*Effective Visualization Techniques*

To use visualization effectively, start by clearly defining your goal. Close your eyes and imagine yourself achieving that goal in vivid detail. Engage all your senses - imagine what you would see, hear, feel, and even smell or taste in that moment of success. Visualize yourself overcoming any obstacles that stand in your way and experiencing the emotions of accomplishment and joy that come with achieving your goal.

*Using Affirmations to Support Positive Thinking*

Repetition of encouraging comments to oneself serves as an affirmation, promoting positive attitudes and beliefs. Affirmations can help counteract negative self-talk and build your confidence and self-esteem. Choose affirmations that resonate with you and reflect the positive outcomes you want to experience in your life. Repeat these affirmations regularly, either silently or out loud, to yourself.

*Examples of Affirmations for Different Aspects of Life*

For health: "I am strong and healthy, and my body is capable of healing itself."

For relationships: "I am surrounded by love and support, and my relationships are fulfilling and harmonious."

For career: "I am successful in all my endeavors, and I attract opportunities for growth and advancement."

By incorporating visualization and affirmations into your daily routine, you can reprogram your subconscious mind to support your goals and dreams. These powerful techniques can help you maintain a positive mindset and stay motivated as you work towards creating the life you desire.

# CHAPTER SIX

# *Overcoming Obstacles to Positive Thinking*

While cultivating a positive mindset can bring many benefits, there are common obstacles that can hinder your efforts. In this chapter, we'll explore these obstacles and provide strategies for overcoming them.

*Common Obstacles to Positive Thinking*

Negative Self-Talk: The inner critic can be a significant barrier to positive thinking. It's important to recognize when negative self-talk is occurring and challenge these thoughts with positive
affirmations.

Fear and Doubt: Fear of failure or doubt in your abilities can prevent you from thinking positively. Practice self-compassion and remind yourself that failure is a natural part of growth.

Comparison: Comparing yourself to others can lead to feelings of inadequacy and negativity. Pay attention to your path and acknowledge every step forward, no matter how tiny.

Past Experiences: Negative experiences from the past can create a negative mindset. Practice forgiveness, both for yourself and others, and focus on the present moment.

*Strategies for Overcoming Negative Thinking Patterns*

Cognitive Restructuring: Replace negative thoughts with more positive and realistic ones. For instance, consider thinking, "I can learn from this experience and improve," as opposed to, "I'll never be able to do this."

Reframing: Look at situations from a different perspective. Consider a setback as a chance to learn and improve rather than as a sign of failure.

Gratitude Practice: Focus on what you're grateful for to shift your focus from what's lacking to what you have.

Positive Affirmations: Use positive affirmations to counteract negative self-talk and build your self-esteem.

*Building Resilience in the Face of Challenges*

The capacity to overcome obstacles and adjust to change is resilience. To build resilience, focus on developing a growth mindset, which sees challenges as opportunities for growth rather than obstacles. Practice self-care, maintain a strong support network, and stay optimistic about the future.

By recognizing and addressing these obstacles, you can cultivate a more positive mindset and overcome challenges with grace and resilience.

# CHAPTER SEVEN

# *Nurturing a Positive Lifestyle*

In this chapter, we'll explore how lifestyle factors can impact your mindset and overall positivity. We'll discuss the importance of self-care, healthy habits, and stress management in maintaining a positive lifestyle.

*The Impact of Lifestyle Factors on Positivity*

Your lifestyle choices, such as diet, exercise, sleep, and social interactions, can significantly impact your mindset. A healthy lifestyle can help you feel more energized, optimistic, and resilient, while an unhealthy lifestyle can lead to feelings of fatigue, stress, and negativity.

*How to Develop Positive Habits in Your Everyday Life*

*Regular Physical Activity*: Exercise is not only good for your physical health but also your mental health. It can elevate your general well-being, lessen stress, and lift your spirits.

*Healthy Eating Habits*: A balanced diet rich in fruits, vegetables, whole grains, and lean proteins can help support your mood and energy levels. Avoiding excessive sugar, caffeine, and processed foods can also help maintain a more stable mood.

*Adequate Sleep*: Sleep is something that sometimes gets overlooked however, lack of sleep can lead to irritability, stress, and difficulty maintaining a positive mindset. Therefore, it is very essential to give our body the rest it needs to function by getting good quality sleep.

*Social Connections*: Spending time with friends and loved ones can boost your mood and provide a sense of belonging and support. Try to nurture your relationships and engage in social activities regularly.

*The Importance of Self-Care and Stress Management*

Self-care is about taking time to prioritize your physical, emotional, and mental well-being. This can include activities such as meditation, yoga, reading, or simply taking a walk-in nature. Stress management techniques, such as deep breathing, progressive muscle relaxation, or mindfulness meditation, can also help reduce stress and promote a more positive outlook on life.

By incorporating these positive habits into your daily life, you can nurture a positive lifestyle that supports your overall well-being and helps you maintain a positive mindset even during challenging times. Remember, small changes can lead to big improvements in your mood and outlook on life.

# CHAPTER EIGHT

# *The Power of Positive Thinking in Action*

In this chapter, we'll explore real-life examples and case studies that demonstrate the transformative power of positive thinking. These stories illustrate how individuals have overcome adversity, achieved their goals, and transformed their lives through the power of positivity.

*Case Study: Overcoming Adversity*

Sarah was a vibrant young woman with a promising career ahead of her when she was diagnosed with a chronic illness that threatened to derail her life. Initially, Sarah felt overwhelmed and defeated, unsure of how she would cope with the challenges that lay ahead. However, she was determined not to let her illness define her.

Sarah began researching her condition and exploring ways to manage her symptoms. She discovered the power of positive thinking and decided to adopt a more optimistic outlook on life. She started practicing gratitude for the small victories, such as being able to get out of bed in the morning or enjoy a meal with friends. She also began visualizing a future where she was healthy and thriving, focusing on the life she wanted to create rather than the challenges she faced.

Over time, Sarah's health began to improve. She found that by focusing on the positive aspects of her life, she was better able to manage her illness and its symptoms. Today, Sarah is living a full and active life, pursuing her passions and dreams, all thanks to her positive mindset and determination to overcome adversity.

*Case Study: Achieving Goals*

John had always dreamed of starting his own business, but he lacked the confidence and clarity to take the first step. He was overwhelmed by the challenges and uncertainties that lay ahead and doubted whether he had what it took to succeed. However, John was determined not to let fear hold him back.

John began practicing positive affirmations, telling himself that he was capable, resourceful, and deserving of success. He also started visualizing his business thriving, imagining himself serving his customers and making a positive impact on his community. These practices helped boost John's confidence and motivation, enabling him to take small, actionable steps towards his goal.

Despite setbacks along the way, John persevered. He sought guidance from mentors, learned from his mistakes, and adapted his approach as needed. Today, John runs a successful business that he's passionate about, serving his community and living out his dream, all thanks to his positive mindset and determination to achieve his goals.

*Case Study: Transforming Relationships*

Maria was feeling disconnected from her loved ones and constantly at odds with her colleagues at work. She was frustrated by the lack of understanding and empathy in her relationships and longed for deeper, more meaningful connections. However, Maria realized that in order to change her relationships, she first had to change herself.

Maria began practicing active listening, trying to truly understand the perspectives and feelings of others. She also focused on finding common ground, seeking out shared interests and experiences that could bridge the gap between them. Maria also used positive affirmations to strengthen her relationships, reminding herself that she was capable of empathy, understanding, and forgiveness.

As a result of her efforts, Maria's relationships began to improve significantly. She found that by approaching her relationships with positivity and empathy, she was able to build deeper connections with others and cultivate a more positive and supportive environment both at home and at work. Today, Mara enjoys fulfilling relationships with her loved ones and colleagues, all thanks to her positive mindset and willingness to transform her relationships.

# CHAPTER NINE

# *Embracing a Positive Future*

In this final chapter, we'll explore how you can continue to cultivate a positive mindset and incorporate positive thinking into your daily life to create a brighter, more fulfilling future.

*Recap of Key Points*

Throughout this ebook, we've discussed the transformative power of positive thinking and how it can impact every aspect of your life. From improving your mental and physical health to enhancing your relationships and achieving your goals, positive thinking can help you lead a more fulfilling and meaningful life.

*Practical Tips for Maintaining a Positive Mindset*

Practice gratitude daily: Every day, set aside some time to think about your blessings. This can help shift your focus from what's lacking to what you have. Surround yourself with positivity: Surround yourself with positive influences, whether it's uplifting music, inspirational books, or supportive friends and family.

Practice mindfulness: Stay present and focused on the moment. Mindfulness can help you become more aware of your thoughts and feelings, allowing you to choose positive responses.

Set realistic goals: Make sure your goals are both difficult and attainable. This can help keep you motivated and focused on the positive outcomes you want to achieve.

Celebrate your successes: Take time to celebrate your achievements, no matter how small. This can help reinforce positive behaviors and attitudes.

*Looking Ahead*

As you continue on your journey of positive thinking, remember that it's a lifelong practice. There will be times when negativity creeps in, but the key is to acknowledge these thoughts and refocus on the positive. By cultivating a positive mindset and incorporating positive habits into your daily life, you can create a future filled with

happiness, success, and fulfillment.

In closing, remember that you have the power to shape your own reality through the power of positive thinking. Embrace each day with optimism and gratitude and watch as your life transforms in the way you never thought possible.

# ABOUT THE AUTHOR

Favour Uzoukwu is a nurse whose journey is a testament to resilience and determination. Born into humble beginnings, she faced numerous challenges on her path to becoming a nurse, including financial hardships and personal setbacks. Through sheer grit and perseverance, Favour worked tirelessly to put herself through school, never losing sight of her dream. Today, as a dedicated nurse, she continues to inspire others with her compassionate care and unwavering commitment to improving the lives of those around her. Her story is a reminder that with perseverance and a positive mindset, anything is possible.

9 798884 293458